THE BASICS OF

PERFORMANCE MEASUREMENT

JERRY L. HARBOUR, Ph.D.

QUALITY RESOURCES.
A Division of The Kraus Organization Limited
New York, New York

Most Quality Resources books are available at quantity discounts when purchased in bulk. For more information contact:

Special Sales Department
Quality Resources
A Division of The Kraus Organization Limited
902 Broadway
New York, NY   10010
212-979-8600
800-247-8519

Printed in the United States of America

08 07 06 05 04   10 9 8 7 6 5 4 3 2

ISBN 0-527-76328-4

Contents

CHAPTER 1

Performance Measurement

*You can't improve what you
can't (or don't) measure.*

Whether we use process improvement, process reengineering,
Kaizen, just-in-time, activity-based costing, total quality management, continuous quality improvement, or cycle time
reduction, we share one basic goal: to do more better and faster
with less. A critical enabler in each of these endeavors is the
ability to measure performance. As the saying goes, *"You can't
improve what you can't (or don't) measure."*

A critical enabler in achieving desired
performance goals is the ability to measure
performance.

How would you respond, for example, if the CEO of your company challenged you to cut the average cycle time of a particular process by 50 percent over the next 12 months? One

possible avenue would be to brainstorm a few ideas and implement one or two. At the end of the 12-month period, you could then go back to the CEO and assure him that indeed, cycle time had been cut in half. If the discerning CEO happened to ask you for some positive proof to back up your assertion, you might be surprised—wasn't it obvious? No longer is "obviousness" enough. Standards such as ISO 9000, for example, require documentation of such improvements.

A different and more defensible approach to the CEO's challenge would be to:

- *First establish the baseline cycle time of the current process.* That is, you would measure the "as is"—in this case, say, current average cycle time is 8 days.
- *Next calculate half.* This would determine your actual goal for the coming year. In this case, four days, which now becomes your targeted goal.
- *Determine the gap or delta between the current cycle time and targeted cycle time.* To reach your desired goal, you must somehow eliminate four days from the present process.
- *Develop and implement a process improvement solution.*
- *Finally throughout the year, perhaps on a monthly basis, remeasure the current cycle time.* Such periodic measures help you track the progress you are hopefully making toward achieving the desired four-day goal.

At the end of the year, you can graphically show the CEO your progress with a chart like the one illustrated in Figure 1. You could state that 12 months ago, the average cycle time was eight days. You would then show the CEO the monthly progress chart and proudly announce that the current cycle

Figure 1. Performance Measurement Graph

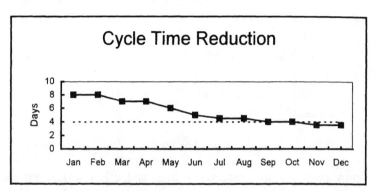

A performance-related graph depicting decreasing cycle time over a 12-month period.

time is 3.5 days. This actually represents a 56 percent reduction in cycle time, rather than the targeted 50 percent!

The first approach, common in the past, is based on opinion and speculation. The second is based on fact and actual measurement. Increasingly, companies are opting for the latter approach. They are managing their improvement efforts based on fact. And those facts are being derived by measuring performance. That is, companies are using performance measurements to help achieve desired performance levels.

Companies are discovering that performance measures can help any organization:

- Determine where they are — that is, establish an initial baseline "as is" performance level.
- Establish goals based on their current performance.
- Determine the gap or delta between a set of desired goals and current performance levels.

- Track progress in achieving desired performance goals.
- Compare and benchmark their competitors' performance levels with their own.
- Control performance levels within predetermined boundaries.
- Identify problem areas and possible problem causes.
- Better plan for the future.

The insights gained from systematically measuring performance can be truly amazing. One company, for example, had previously spent considerable time and effort measuring its production process, focusing especially on the related performance measures of cost and cycle time. Unfortunately, however, they had completely ignored the associated distribution process that accompanied the production process.

Finally, they began to put in place baseline and trending measures that could capture total enterprise performance, from initial production through final distribution. Distribution was defined as beginning when the product left the production line and ending when it was physically unloaded at the customer's receiving dock. Of great importance to the company, it was only at this final end point (representing actual receipt of the product) that the company was "physically" paid.

Once the company began to measure the performance of the total enterprise, they were astounded at what they found. The production portion of total product cycle time measured only about 11 percent, which translated into approximately two weeks. Some 90 percent of total product cycle time (representing over three months) was tied up in distribution. That is, they had a finished product, which theoretically could be transformed into cash, that was spending an inexorable amount of time in an "unpaid" distribution pipeline.

Realizing the situation, the company quickly took steps to shorten cycle time associated with distribution. They also established additional performance measures that would carefully monitor all aspects of the distribution process. The immediate result was an increase in cash flow, since the company could now more quickly collect on its products. Looking back, one rather irritated top manager wanted to know why the situation had existed so long without being corrected. Although many excuses were made, in the end it simply reinforced the axiom that you can't improve what you can't (or don't) measure.

In essence, measuring performance can help drive desired results at any level—organizationwide, departmental, or process. Before discussing performance measurement further, however, we should first define some important concepts.

**Measuring performance can help drive
desired business results.**

KEY CONCEPTS AND DEFINITIONS

Some key concepts and definitions relating to performance measurement include:

- *Baseline performance.* This is the current level at which an organization, process, or function is performing. A company currently producing 25 units per week has a current baseline performance of 25 units per week.

- *Family of measures.* This represents a group of usually four to six interrelated but still separate key aspects (or family members) of performance. Key types of measures within a family of measures typically include:

— Productivity measurements (e.g., 25 units produced per week).
— Quality measurements (e.g., 3.8 defects per 25 units).
— Timeliness measurements (e.g., 96 percent of orders completed on time).
— Cycle time measurements (e.g., a production cycle time of 6 hours per unit).
— Resource utilization measurements (e.g., production workers utilized 65 percent of the time).
— Cost measurements (e.g., production cost of $325 per unit).

• *In-process performance measure.* This is a performance measure collected within a process. For example, if a process is comprised of three major activities, the cycle time of each individual activity would be an example of an in-process performance measurement. So would the number of generated defects associated with each individual activity.

• *Key performance factors.* These performance variables are especially critical in achieving a desired set of outcomes. Key performance factors are normally linked to core products and services and associated customer expectations. For example, in a service industry, timeliness, quality, and cost represent three key performance factors.

• *Performance.* An actual work accomplishment or output. In this context performance should not be confused with work behavior. Performance focuses on an actual accomplishment or produced output. Some suggest that performance is what's left behind at the end of the work day. An example of a performance accomplishment is processing 50 procurement requisitions in a single day.

- *Performance goal.* This is a targeted level of accomplishment expressed as a tangible and measurable objective against which actual achievement is compared. For example, a performance goal may be to process, on average, 60 procurement requisitions per day.
- *Performance indicator.* This is a comparative performance metric used to answer the question, "How are we doing?" for a specific issue. The average number of requisitions processed per day is an example of a performance indicator.
- *Performance measure hierarchy.* This is when the same performance measure (e.g., cycle time) is tailored to different user needs at different levels within an organization. For example, whereas front-line supervisors are probably most interested in the cycle time of their own particular activity, the general manager is interested in the total cycle time of all combined activities.
- *Performance measurement.* This is the process of measuring work accomplishments and output, as well as measuring in-process parameters that affect work output and accomplishments. Measuring the cycle time of a service process would be an example of taking a performance measurement.
- *Performance measurement system.* This is normally a graphical and numerical information system used to achieve desired performance levels. A performance measurement system involves the collection, synthesis, delivery, and display of information related to the measurement of work output and accomplishments, as well as in-process parameters that affect work output and accomplishments. All of the varying elements of an organization's performance measurement program comprise a performance measurement system.

- *Performance metric.* This is a specific performance measurement such as cycle time or quality yield.
- *Process.* This represents the transformation and blending of a set of inputs into a more valuable set of outputs. Outputs can be products, services, or accomplished tasks. A process can be further subdivided into a series of interrelated activities. Activities in turn can be subdivided into individual process steps (e.g., operation, transportation, delay, inspections, storage, and rework). Processing insurance claims or providing healthcare in a hospital are both examples of a process.

SUMMARY

Increasingly, companies are moving from management by opinion to management by fact—that is, away from a soft science approach to performance measurement. Instead, they are collecting hard numbers and using those numbers to set and achieve desired performance levels. A key enabler in this transition is the development of a performance measurement system. The goal of any performance measurement system is to provide the right people with the right performance-related information at the right time. One highly successful service company, for example, has developed a real-time computer-based performance system that can collect and distribute a number of performance measures, depicting how rapidly the company is responding to various customer requests. Armed with this information, the company can make on-the-spot adjustments in work assignments to ensure customers are receiving the highest levels of service possible.

CHAPTER 2

Types of Performance Measures

Don't measure what you can't or won't use.

Most companies collect performance measures. Unfortunately, a large percentage of those companies rarely, if ever, use them. Instead, they make an attractive performance indicator display on some obscure wall and then basically ignore the collected data altogether.

The reality is, collecting performance measures takes real effort and time, and time costs real dollars. If collected performance measures are not going to be used and simply ignored, why collect them in the first place?

The key to successful performance measurement is to collect only those performance measures that can or will actually be used. The first step in this process is to determine what types of performance-related information are actually needed to better run and manage an organization, department, or process. That is, to complete the statement, "I need performance-related information in order to...." For example, I need performance-related information in order to better track how long it takes to fill customer orders. Knowing such performance-related information can help us identify which measures to collect. It can also help us identify who the right people are to receive the information and when it is required.

The key to collecting performance measures
is to identify those measures that will actually
help achieve desired results and then deliver
them to the right people at the right time.

Performance measures can be used for a number of different purposes. Such purposes can range from determining current performance levels to predicting future ones to carefully controlling an existing process. In some instances, a single performance metric, such as cycle time, can serve multiple purposes. In other instances, a particular performance metric, such as queue time for a single operation, may have only a very limited, but still important use. The following section describes some general types and uses of performance measures. In chapter 3, specific types of performance measures are identified and discussed under the concept of a family of measures.

USES OF PERFORMANCE MEASURES

As noted, performance measures can be used for multiple purposes. Some general types of performance measures are discussed in the following sections.

Baseline Performance Measures

Baseline measurements are some of the most important measures that can ever be gathered. They answer the question,

"Where am I starting from?" That is, they establish a baseline for current performance, forming the basis for all subsequent measures. As illustrated in Figure 2, which displays the average cycle time of process X, a baseline measure is the first point on the graph. In this instance, it is eight days.

Figure 2. Initial Baseline Measurement

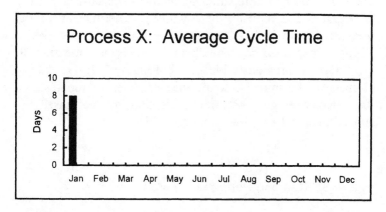

An initial baseline measurement, which in this case is eight days.

Collecting initial baseline measures usually represents lots of hard work—especially for processes that have never been measured before—but such initial efforts are critical to the development and success of any performance measurement system or performance improvement effort. No baseline measures essentially means no performance measurement system, and you can't improve what you can't measure. So always start with collecting baseline measures, establishing a starting point to compare subsequent changes or improvements against.

A baseline measure answers the question,
"Where am I starting from?"

Trending Performance Measures

A trending performance measure shows how something is
doing over time by comparing something — usually an activity, output, or accomplishment — with a predetermined baseline
measure. Figure 3 plots average processing cycle time over a
12-month period. It begins with an initial baseline measure of
eight days, as previously illustrated in Figure 2. It then tracks
changes in the initial baseline measure over 12 months. As
illustrated, average processing cycle time has decreased by
about 50 percent over the 12-month period.

Figure 3. Trending Performance Measures

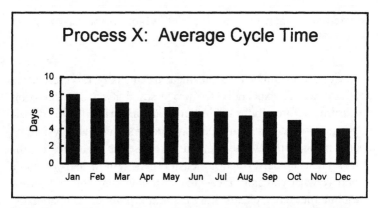

Trending measures illustrating decreasing average cycle
times for process X over a 12-month period.

Such trending measures can quickly highlight specific performance levels over a specified time period. Comparing trending measures with an initial baseline measure, in this instance, quickly answers the question "How have we been doing in our cycle time reduction effort over the last 12 months?"

A trending measure shows how
something is doing over time.

Control Performance Measures

A control performance measure (often in the form of a control chart) answers the question, "Am I staying within some predetermined boundary or tolerance?" Usually used as rapid feedback measures, control measures provide early warnings that something is starting to stray from a predetermined or required performance level. For example, an organization may determine that six defects per production run is the maximum tolerable number of defects. The control chart illustrated in Figure 4, would alert managers to a potential problem with the number of defects.

If it is important to keep a process within predetermined levels, then you need control performance measures. As described in chapter 5, control performance measures must often be collected in almost real time. This information in turn must be provided immediately to the people directly performing a specific task. Control measures are usually of little use or value after the fact.

A control measure shows whether you are
staying within some predetermined boundary.

Figure 4. A Typical Control Chart

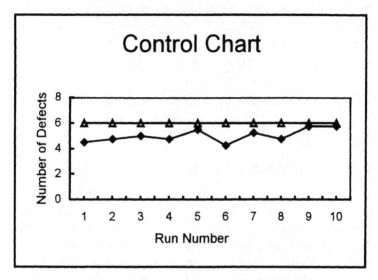

A typical control chart. Note in this example that all control points are within predetermined upper and lower limits.

Diagnostic Performance Measures

Frequently, performance problems are identified through performance measurement. Although you can't improve what you can't measure, sometimes you also can't even identify what's wrong unless you measure. For example, in Figure 5, trending data indicates that average processing cycle time is suddenly and unexpectedly increasing, not continuing to decrease as expected. In such instances, the question "Why?" arises. This is usually followed by the question, "Where is the problem area?" A diagnostic measure provides the answers. It attempts to orient you to a specific problem area. In many instances,

Figure 5. Sample Performance Chart Showing an
            Increase in Average Cycle Times

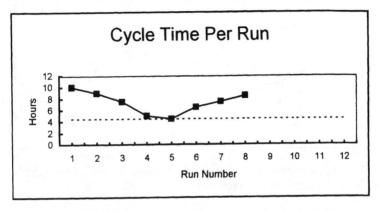

A performance chart illustrating decreasing cycle times
which suddenly begin increasing after production run #5.

trending or control performance measures can also serve as
diagnostic measures.

Assume that the process illustrated in Figure 5 is composed of three major activities (1, 2, and 3). Also assume that
cycle time data is collected for each of these three activities.
This information is in turn combined to create the graph
depicted in Figure 5. Examining each of these three activity-
related cycle time graphs, as illustrated in Figure 6, quickly
identifies that the recent increase in cycle time is associated
with activity 3. That is, the performance measures help *diagnose* where the problem resides, so instead of asking, "What is
causing cycle time to suddenly increase?" we can be more specific. We are able to ask, "What is causing cycle time to
increase in activity 3?"

Figure 6. Activity-Related Cycle Time Graphs

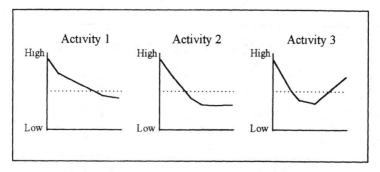

Graphs depicting activity-specific average cycle times. Note sharp increase associated with Activity #3

Additional time-related measures may be able to narrow the problem area down even further. For example, if average processing delay times are being trended for specific operations within activity 3, we may be able to determine that operation Y in particular is causing problems. Having the performance-related information illustrated in Figures 6 and 7, we can now be even more specific in our questioning. We are able to ask, "Why are processing delay times associated with operation Y in activity 3 increasing?" Armed with this kind of information, subsequent corrective efforts can be better focused on the actual problem area.

Such diagnostic measures can also help prevent a problem from occurring in the first place. One service company for example, tracks the amount of time it takes to respond to specific customer requests. At any time of the day, front-line supervisors can immediately access a computer system to see how customer requests are queuing up. They can instantly determine the amount of time that has elapsed on any given

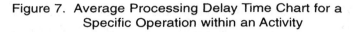

Figure 7. Average Processing Delay Time Chart for a
Specific Operation within an Activity

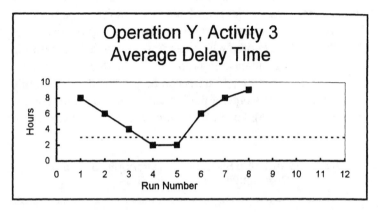

Delay times associated with Operation Y of Activity #3.
Note sharp increases in delay times after run #5.

request. If an unacceptable backlog is beginning to accumulate, supervisors can quickly shift requests around to other workers. This computer-based performance tracking system greatly helps supervisors meet the company's self-imposed time deadlines. It also helps ensure happy customers. In this example, a diagnostic measure is also used as a control measure and vice versa.

> A diagnostic measure helps identify
> where the problem area is.

Planning Performance Measures

All organizations must plan, both on a micro and macro level. Having "hard" data to assist them in their planning efforts is invaluable. Planning performance measurements are predictive measures. They answer the question, "Given certain information and past performance levels, what can I plan for in the future?"

Figure 8, for example, plots the relationship between productivity and cycle time where decreases in cycle time result in a corresponding increase in productivity. With a cycle time of four days, for example, 32 units can be produced on a monthly basis. Knowing this type of performance-related information, a production planning level of 384 units (12 x 32) per year could be projected.

Figure 8. Chart Showing the Relationship between
          Productivity and Cycle Time

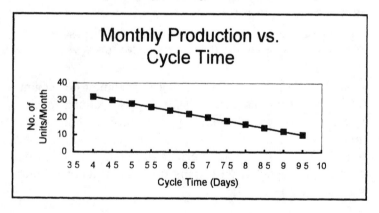

A comparative graph between production and cycle time. The graph illustrates that as cycle time decreases, productivity increases in a linear fashion.

Such measurement- or fact-based information also allows a company to more intelligently develop various what-if scenarios. In the previous example, the company may not want to produce 32 units per month. Instead, they may decide to produce only 16 units. They could then use the perofrmance-related information to determine the number of work crews required to produce the smaller output.

Performance measures take much of the guesswork out of the planning function because the best indicator of future performance levels is often a measured record of past performance levels and associated trends.

A planning measure answers the question, "Given certain information and past performance levels, what can I predict and plan for in the future?"

SUMMARY

Performance measures can be used for a number of different purposes and can answer a number of different types of questions. Such questions can include:

- What is the current performance level (a baseline measure)?
- How is a specific performance level changing over time (a trending measure)?
- Is performance staying within some predetermined boundary or tolerance level (a control measure)?
- What's causing a specific problem and where is the problem area located (a diagnostic measure)?
- Given past and current performance levels, what levels should be planned for in the future (a planning measure)?

Again, the various types of performance measures are not mutually exclusive. For example, a trending measure can also be used as a diagnostic or as even a planning measure.

By initially assessing what performance-related information needs exist, as well as better understanding how such information will or can be used, a performance measurement system can be better designed, implemented, and maintained.

Creating a Performance Measurement System

Step	Description
1	Define needed types of performance-related information that can help achieve desired performance levels.

CHAPTER 3

A Family of Measures

Measure the critical few,
not the trivial many.

Every organization wants to achieve the highest levels of performance possible. Yet to do so almost always requires a delicate balancing act of all the variables that affect performance. Few if any companies, for example, can afford to focus solely on quality while completely ignoring cost, productivity, or cycle time. Instead, they must divide their efforts among these critical performance factors so that optimum — but not necessarily equal — amounts of time are spent on each. Because companies must work with a number of key performance variables, a single measure of performance is rarely adequate. Rather, a family of measures is required.

Companies must attempt to optimize a key set
of performance variables.

Think for a moment about your car's dashboard. Grouped in front of you is a series of measures that represent key performance factors related to the task of driving a car. Usually there are about six performance measure displays — a speedometer, odometer, tachometer, fuel gauge, temperature gauge, and oil pressure gauge. You really need each of these, not just one. Although only having a speedometer may help keep you from getting a ticket, it won't prevent you from running out of gas. Nor will it let you know that your engine is overheating or how far you've traveled. The various measures represented on your dashboard, although interrelated, still provide separate types of required information.

We could certainly add many more driving-related measurements as well. In fact, we could easily place gauges everywhere. This would provide an array of performance-related information. For example, we could have a gauge showing the number of "dings" in the car's body. Or we could have a gauge indicating that both bumpers are still firmly attached. The list could be almost endless. Yet with such a cumbersome array, could we easily identify what's important to the core task of driving a car — the critical few?

Many companies take the same approach in developing a performance measurement system. They try to measure everything and in the process, they dilute what's really important. One company for example found itself collecting more than 100 different performance measures. Yet they found that they really weren't using any of them. Finally in frustration, they completely junked their existing performance measurement system. The company now collects only a handful of critical measures, focusing their efforts on the *critical few instead of the trivial many*. These critical few measures represent what is commonly termed a *family of measures*.

The concept of a family of measures is normally associated with the excellent work of Carl G. Thor (see *Further Reading*). As noted in chapter 1, a family of measures usually represents four to six interrelated but still separate key aspects of performance. A family of measures captures key activities and outputs of critical importance to an organization. Such measures are normally linked to core products and services, customer expectations, or an organization's mission and associated enabling objectives. In many instances, multiple measures of the same family member are collected. For example, various timeliness-related measures may be collected within the same organization.

Ideally, a short scan of a family of measures can quickly and concisely provide anyone with a good overview of how well an organization is performing. A family of measures basically serves as a performance snapshot.

KEY CHARACTERISTICS

The following sections describe what a family of measures should do.

Accurately measure key performance variables.

A family of measures typically incorporates the following types of measures:

- *Productivity.* This is usually expressed as the relationship between the physical inputs and outputs of a defined process. That is, the relationship between the number of outputs versus the resources consumed in producing those outputs. Frequently, a productivity measure answers the questions, "How much?" or "How many?" An example of a productivity measure is 55 units produced by a four-person work crew in one week.

- *Quality.* This commonly includes both internal measurements like scrap, number of rejects, and defects per unit, as well as external customer satisfaction ratings or customer repeat frequencies.

- *Timeliness.* This pertains to things like percentage of on-time deliveries or percentage of orders shipped when promised. Basically, timeliness measures assess whether you're doing what you say you're going to do *when* you say you'll do it.

- *Cycle time.* This refers to the amount of time it takes to proceed from one defined point in a process to another. A cycle time measurement measures how long something takes. For example, a typical cycle time measurement may be the amount of time on average it takes from when a customer places an order to when the customer actually receives the order.

- *Resource utilization.* This is a measurement of resources used versus resources available for use. Resource utilization can apply to such things as machines, computers, vehicles, and even people. A labor resource utilization rate of 40 percent indicates that personnel are being productively utilized only 40 percent of the time they are available for work. By knowing utilization rates, an organization may find that it doesn't really need more resources. Instead, it just needs to better utilize the ones they already have!

- *Costs.* This is especially useful if calculated on a per unit basis. For example, a particular service costs a company $16 each time it is performed. Somewhat surprising, many companies have little information on per unit costs.

Depending on the setting, there are certainly other types of performance-related measurements that can be included in a family of measures. Safety, as expressed in the number of accidents per so many hundreds or thousands of hours, is important in all industrial settings. Perhaps the best advice is to measure what's important and use these measures to help achieve desired performance levels.

> Measure what's important, using what's
> measured to help achieve desired
> performance levels.

As previously noted, in some instances, a company may develop multiple measures of a single family member. One highly successful service company for example, focuses on rapidly responding to its customers. Indeed the company has discovered, as have many other service companies, that customer response time is a critical success factor in maintaining continued customer loyalty. Fortunately, the company currently has a very loyal customer base. Unfortunately, such premium customers demand good service and they demand it immediately. As a consequence, the company has developed some 15 performance measures, many of them relating to speed of response in dealing with customer requests and needs. Some of their speed of response measures relating to timeliness include:

- Percentage of customer address changes processed within one day.
- Percentage of telephone calls from customers picked up within two rings.
- Percentage of calls coming to the switchboard transferred to the appropriate party within 21 seconds.
- Percentage of increased credit line approvals for basic customers completed within 30 minutes and for so-called platinum customers within 15 minutes.

Include a comparative basis to assist in better understanding displayed performance levels.

Examine Figure 9 carefully. Then try to answer the question, "How well is this aspect of the process performing?" Basically you can't, because you have nothing to compare the numbers with. A speedometer that reads 50 mph, for instance, can't tell you whether you are going too fast, too slow, or just right unless you also know the posted speed limit for the road you're traveling on.

It's important then when developing a family of measures to also have a means of bringing meaning to the measurements. Figure 10 illustrates the same graph presented in Figure 9. However, Figure 10 now includes a production goal represented by a dashed line that quickly and clearly indicates that production levels are predominantly falling short of the desired goal set by the company. The company is either experiencing a serious production problem or has set some very unrealistic or unachievable goals for itself.

Figure 9. Production Graph with No Comparative Information

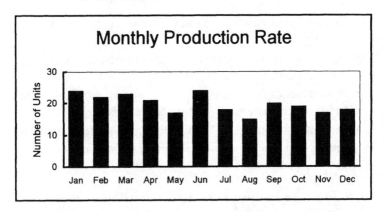

A graph depicting monthly production rates. From the graph, however, there is no way of determining if these performance levels are acceptable.

Figure 10. Production Graph Including Comparative
Information

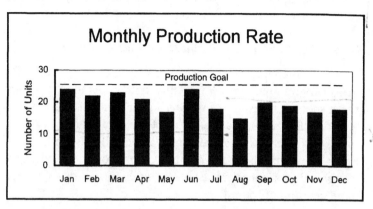

The same graph as illustrated in Figure 9. However in
this case, a dashed "goal" line has been inserted, reveal-
ing that production rates have fallen below the planned
goal each month.

Be collected and distributed on a timely basis.

This is discussed in more detail in chapter 5, but basically, to
be usable, measurement collection and distribution frequencies
must be driven by user needs. It wouldn't do much good for
example, to have your car's speedometer only "come on" for
five seconds every five minutes. While driving, you must be
able to monitor your speed almost continuously. That is, you
must have a continuous performance measurement display system at your immediate disposal. Increasingly, as business trans-
actions speed up, performance measures must be collected and
displayed at the same near real-time frequency. This near real-
time need, however, places severe demands on any performance measurement collection and distribution system.

Fortunately in many instances, computer-based systems can permit the rapid collection, distribution, and display of needed performance-related information.

Be analyzable on both a macro and micro basis.

As noted in chapter 2, performance measures can be used for many different purposes. Frequently, both in-depth information about specific measures as well as bigger picture overviews are required. By creating a hierarchy of the same family of measures, performance measurements can be rolled-up to a higher level. They can also be decomposed for more detailed information. Performance measure hierarchies are described in more detail in chapter 4.

Cannot be easily manipulated to achieve desired results.

In selecting a set of performance measures, make sure that they cannot be easily manipulated by someone to achieve desired results. Selecting measures that are true indicators of core performance will usually prevent such creative accounting systems. Performance measures often control or influence human behavior. Just make sure that they are influencing the right types of behavior.

One company, for example, launched a plantwide process improvement program. Top management decided to carefully track the number of performance improvement teams chartered within each division and the number of meetings each team held. They thought these traits represented good performance indicators for what they called division commitment. However, no measures of actual accomplishment were ever instituted. As such, some crafty division managers simply launched lots of teams and had them meet frequently, but only for very short periods of time. Unfortunately, nothing of any substance was ever accomplished in any of the team meetings. Yet the associated performance measures of number of teams launched and frequency of meetings looked great to unsuspecting top management.

The very process of developing a family of performance measures will often help a company focus on what's actually required in order to be successful. Although measuring everything seems nice, such efforts frequently dilute a company's attention to what's really important. Therefore, measure only what's really important and what will actually be used by a real person.

Creating a family of measures will often help an organization focus on what's important.

CORRELATED MEASURES

As noted in chapter 2, collecting performance measures takes real effort and time, which costs any organization real dollars. Therefore, it's important to collect only those measures that provide the greatest information and are most usable. In some instances, two (or more) performance measures may be very closely related or correlated with each other. In such instances, it makes little sense to collect both measures in a family of measures. Instead, simply collect one measure and extrapolate the collected information to the other measure if needed.

Correlation refers to the degree of relatedness between two (or more) variables. Performance measures can be either positively or negatively correlated. A positive correlation means that as one variable increases or decreases, another variable also increases or decreases in the same fashion. A negative correlation describes two variables that are inversely related. As one increases, the other decreases. Correlations can range from 0 (essentially no correlation) to 1.0 (a perfect correlation).

Cycle time and labor costs are a good example of two performance measures that are often highly correlated. If for example, you are collecting cycle time data and cycle time is essentially composed of labor hours, you only need labor rates to calculate actual labor costs. That is, one performance measure, in this instance cycle time, can give you a second measure — cost — without going to the effort of directly collecting cost data.

It is essential then when developing a family of measures to make sure that two or more of the measures aren't directly correlated to each other. If they are, collect only one performance measure and simply extrapolate to the other if needed. A family of measures should contain separate measures that aren't closely correlated.

Every organization is somewhat unique. Therefore, an organization's specific family of performance measures should reflect this uniqueness. That is, they should be custom fitted to the organization's particular needs. As noted, a family of measures typically involves the following types of individual measures:

- Productivity measures.
- Quality measures.
- Timeliness measures (e.g., on-time deliveries).
- Cycle time measures.
- Resource utilization measures.
- Cost measures.

Some examples of specific measures that might be included in a family of measures from different business and industrial sectors are:

- *Accounting-related performance measures:*
    - — Number of errors reported by outside auditors.
    - — Payroll processing cycle time.
    - — Billing (preparation and sending) cycle time.
    - — Credit application approval cycle time.
    - — Average number of days from receipt to processing.
- *Customer service-related performance measures:*
    - — Percentage of calls coming to the switchboard transferred to the appropriate party within x seconds.
    - — Average cycle time to process customer request or service order.
    - — Average queue times.
    - — Customer repeat frequency.
    - — Number of customer service-related complaints.
- *Engineering-related performance measures:*
    - — Number of design change notices per engineering project.
    - — Engineer labor utilization.
    - — Number of drawing errors per design sheet.
    - — Percentage of total design time used for redesign.
    - — Percentage of on-time drawing release.
- *Healthcare-related performance measures (relating to operating theaters):*
    - — Average cycle time of operating theater turnaround and/or changeover.
    - — Cost of materials per operation.
    - — Operating theater utilization rates.
    - — Percentage of delays due to unavailable resources (e.g., personnel, equipment, or supplies).
- *Information systems-related performance measures:*
    - — Percentage of customer problems not corrected per schedule.

— Mean time between system interruptions.
— Mean time between system repairs.
— Rework costs resulting from computer programs.
— Average response time to help desk complaints.

• *Mail order service-related performance measures:*
  — Percentage of orders shipped when promised.
  — Average cycle time of customer order to customer receipt.
  — Percentage of orders returned due to service errors.
  — Percentage of total orders back-ordered.
  — Customer satisfaction ratings.

• *Maintenance-related Performance Measures:*
  — Maintenance cost/throughput.
  — Percentage of facility maintenance-related downtime.
  — Call-back frequency for defective maintenance repairs.
  — Percentage of on-time maintenance service commitments.
  — Work order cycle time.
  — Average cycle time of preventive maintenance calls.

• *Manufacturing-related performance measures:*
  — Number of defects per produced unit.
  — Per unit costs.
  — Labor utilization.
  — Percentage of on-time production deliveries.
  — Percentage of manufacturing facility downtime.
  — Changeover cycle times.

• *Procurement/purchasing-related performance measures:*
  — Percentage of supplies delivered per schedule.
  — Purchase order cycle time.
  — Percentage of purchase orders returned due to errors.

- — Number of items on the "hot list."
- — Parts costs per total costs
- *Sales-related performance measures:*
  - — Percentage of return sales.
  - — Percentage of new sales.
  - — Number of sales calls per week or month.
  - — Sales costs versus sale amount.
  - — On-time delivery of sales commitments.
- *Shipping/trucking-related performance measures:*
  - — Total tonnage hauled per road mile.
  - — Percentage of total road miles hauling empty.
  - — Percentage of on-time pickups and deliveries.
  - — Average length of cargo delays at distribution centers.
  - — Accidents per x road miles.
  - — Tickets per x road miles.
  - — Number of breakdowns per x miles.

These examples are by no means intended to represent an exhaustive list. The key in creating performance measurement families is to identify those measures that will actually help someone better manage, control, or improve some aspect of their work. It is also important to stress that when it comes to creating a family of performance measures, more is not always better.

One company for example collected some 24 performance measures on a daily or weekly basis. Over time, the company had established a rather elaborate and costly performance measurement system, headed up by a single department. The company would proudly parade visitors past their performance indicator display boards, positioned strategically throughout the plant, and boast of their value. The elaborate, color-coded displays were indeed striking. The positioned displays followed many of the guidelines for creating good visual displays outlined in chapter 6, *Performance Measure Displays*. To the outside visitor, the company seemed to have an exemplary performance measurement program in place.

Eventually, however, someone within the company asked the question, *"How is each performance measure actually being used?"* The intent of the "mini-audit" was to show the value of each performance measure and how it was specifically being used to support day-to-day operations at the plant.

Surprisingly and of some embarrassment to the company, only 2 of the 24 performance measures were actually being used. Interviewed workers, supervisors, and managers would say things like, "We live by these two indicators. I couldn't do my job without them. But in all honesty, I don't even look at the others. They have no real value to me." They would always add, "I'm sure, however, that someone certainly uses them." Unfortunately, the company never could identify who that someone was for the other 22 performance measures.

Additional comments from the intended users indicated that two other measures that were not being collected, specifically the cycle time and cost of a particular process, would be very beneficial, adding a great deal of value to day-to-day operations. Realizing that an "unused" more may not always be better, the company created a new family of measures consisting of the two measures that were already being used and the two new ones suggested by interviewed employees. A great deal of attention was given to the collection and tracking of these four indicators by almost everyone at the plant. Although the new family of measures meant less work for the department tasked with collecting and displaying performance-related information at the plant, it by no means diminished their value. Indeed the value of the group actually increased.

SUMMARY

In an attempt to focus on the critical few and not the trivial many, some companies use a family of performance measures. A family of measures usually represents four to six interrelated but separate key aspects of performance. A family of measures captures key activities and outputs of critical importance to an organization. As such, they should be directly linked to core products and services, customer expectations, or an organization's primary mission and associated enabling objectives. Normally, a family of measures involves the following types of measures: productivity, quality, timeliness, cycle time, resource utilization, and cost. In many instances, multiple measures of the same family member are collected.

Creating a Performance Measurement System

Step	Description
1	Define needed types of performance-related information that can help achieve desired performance levels.
2	Develop relevant and usable family of measures.

CHAPTER 4

Performance Measurement Hierarchies

Provide the right level of performance-related information.

In chapter 3, it was noted that rarely if ever can a single performance measure capture all aspects of performance. Instead, the use of a family of measures was suggested. A family of measures commonly represents four to six interrelated but separate key aspects of performance.

Just as no single measure can adequately capture all aspects of performance, rarely can a single level of a specific measure be used throughout an organization. Therefore a hierarchy of the same measure is created. Hierarchies measure a similar aspect of performance, but at different levels within the same organization. A general manager for example, usually requires different levels of performance-related information than do front-line supervisors.

Most organizations require a hierarchy of the same measure, measuring a similar aspect of performance, but at different levels.

Think of the example of turnaround time for a large jetliner at a major airport. One key performance measure of this process is cycle time, since speed and timeliness are critical performance factors in the airline industry. Indeed, getting planes in and out of airports as fast and safe as possible helps ensure that tight schedules are maintained in an efficient manner.

Upon closer examination, the jet turnaround process may be divided into a series of activities, as depicted in Figure 11. Some of the activities are directly related. For example, arriving baggage must first be unloaded before departing baggage can be loaded. The same with passengers. Other activities are relatively independent of each other. Service and flight crews for example, must complete their own set of steps and activities irrespective of passenger and baggage loading and unload-

Figure 11. Jet Turnaround Process Activities

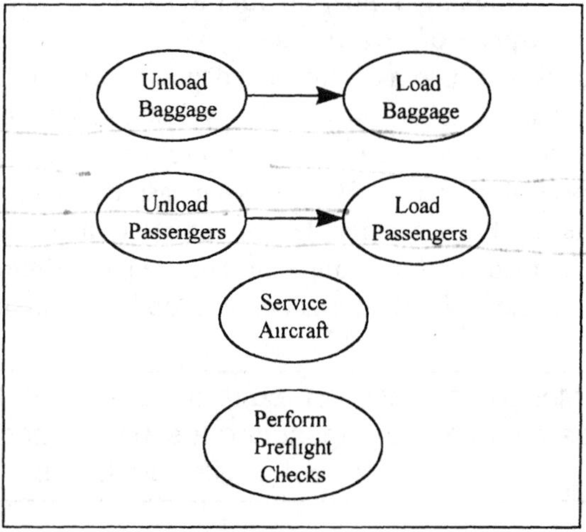

Activities associated with the jet turnaround process. Note that many of the activities are independent of each other.

ing. So must general service and maintenance crews. As such, the process consists of a whole — turning the jet around. It also consists of a series of separate but interrelated activities (e.g., unloading and loading baggage).

Using the jet turnaround process and the performance measure of cycle time as an example, no single cycle time measure is universally applicable or relevant to everyone. Although the total turnaround cycle time may be of great significance to the general manager of operations, it doesn't have the same relevance to the manager of baggage handling. Nor does it have the same meaning to the person overseeing the general servicing of the aircraft. That is, total turnaround cycle time is not a specific enough measure for these two individual activity owners. The baggage manager wants to know how long it takes to get baggage on and off the plane. The person overseeing general servicing wants to know how long fueling and other service-related activities take. To better perform their jobs, they require more specific and relevant cycle time measures than total turnaround cycle time. Although the measure is still the same, that of cycle time, the specific required levels vary.

Tailoring performance measures to individual needs and differing levels of need is sometimes called making performance measures SMART (specific, measurable, action-oriented, relevant, and timely). Different levels of a single performance measure are called a performance measure hierarchy.

Performance measures must be tailored
to individual needs, what some call
making performance measures
SMART (specific, measurable,
action-oriented, relevant, and timely).

A performance measure hierarchy answers the question, "Who needs what level of performance-related information?"

The pyramid chart shown in Figure 12 illustrates a performance measure hierarchy in which lower-level measures are combined to create higher-level measures and higher-level measures are composed of two or more lower-level measures.

Figure 12. A Performance Measure Hierarchy

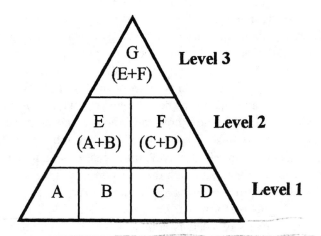

A conceptual, 3-level performance measure hierarchy. In this instance, higher level measures are cumulative of lower level measures.

ADVANTAGES

Creating a hierarchy of the same performance measure has several advantages, including:

- Providing specific and relevant performance-related information to different levels within an organization so that the right people can more easily access the right level of information at the right time. That is, the information becomes more relevant and specific, making it more meaningful and usable as well.

- Collected lower-level measures can be easily combined and rolled up to create higher-level measures. Higher-level measures therefore do not have to be directly measured. Instead, they can simply be summed from previously collected measures.

- A performance measure hierarchy also represents an excellent diagnostic performance measurement system. Higher-level measures can easily be decomposed to lower-level elements when attempting to zero in on a problem area.

A WORD OF CAUTION

When creating a performance measure hierarchy, make sure that associated gaps between separate measures do not exist. For example, preventive maintenance of a particular component may consist of three major activities: Cleaning (activity A), Calibration (activity B), and Testing and Certification (activity C). The three activities occur in a linear fashion. That is, Cleaning occurs before Calibration, and Calibration precedes final Testing and Certification. Further, each activity essentially represents the efforts of a separate department. Let's further assume that each department measures cycle time from when the component is received to when it is shipped to the next department. That is, individual activity cycle time equals exit time minus entrance time.

Using the two-level performance hierarchy concept illustrated in Figure 13, total process cycle time equals the combined cycle times of activities A (Cleaning) + B (Calibration) +

Figure 13. Two-Level Performance Measure Hierarchy

Total
Cycle Time
(A+B+C)   **Level 2**

| A Cycle Time | B Cycle Time | C Cycle Time |

Level 1

A two-level performance measure hierarchy.

C (Testing and Certification). Unfortunately that is in error
because shipping or transportation time between activities and
between activities B and C is missing — that is, it is not being
captured and added to total cycle time. An accurate total cycle
time would equal the sum of the individual cycle times of activities A, B, and C, plus transport times between the various
activities. When creating a performance measure hierarchy,
make sure that such missing gaps are not left out of higher-
level measures.

One way to avoid this common pitfall is to develop performance measures that are process aligned instead of functional-
ly or departmentally aligned. In adopting a process view, all
process elements are captured and measured — even transport
moves between activities. Such measures can then be more easily and accurately rolled-up to higher-level measures.

Avoid creating lower-level performance measures that have associated missing "gaps," which incorrectly roll up to a higher-level performance measure.

SUMMARY

Providing the right level of performance-related information to the right person at the right time is critical for optimizing performance in any organization. In most instances, a hierarchy of differing levels of the same performance measure is required. The creation of a performance hierarchy helps ensure that relevant and meaningful performance-related information is collected and distributed to the right level within an organization.

Creating a Performance Measurement System

Step	Description
1	Define needed types of performance-related information that can help achieve desired performance levels.
2	Develop relevant and usable family of measures.
3	Develop specific performance measurement hierarchies.

CHAPTER 5

Collection and Distribution

Accessibility and timeliness determine performance measure value.

Designing a performance measurement system basically involves answering four types of questions:

- What?
- When?
- Who?
- How?

"What" questions refer to identifying specific types of performance measures to collect. Developing a family of measures and an associated performance measurement hierarchy, as described in chapters 3 and 4 respectively, helps identify what specific measures to gather.

"Who" questions refer to who will actually use the collected performance information. Remember, performance measures must be relevant to a particular individual or group of individuals. All too often, performance measures are collected and never used. It is imperative that actual names of relevant users of the information are specifically identified and associated with each and every performance measure.

In many instances, performance-related information is sent to someone who is merely charged with collecting or assembling the information. This person in turn may send it on to someone else and so forth. Such collectors or "human repositories" do not constitute relevant users. Unless a relevant *user* can be specifically identified by name, collecting a performance measure should be questioned. When developing a performance measurement system, it is often helpful to create a matrix similar to that shown in Figure 14. The matrix pairs at least one user name with each and every proposed performance metric.

> Always associate a specific user name
> with each and every collected
> performance measure.

"When" questions refer to both frequency of collection and timing of distribution. Performance measures can be collected either continuously or on some predetermined intermittent sampling schedule. Continuous collection means that every event is measured. For example, cycle time and number of defects are measured on every manufactured product. Another example of continuous measurement is measuring the timeliness of every filled order.

Collecting performance information on a predetermined intermittent schedule means that only certain events are sampled. For example, cycle time and quality-related information are collected only on every fourth product. Or in filling orders, timeliness is measured only on every tenth order. In determining sample frequency, it is always important to let the needs of the relevant user help dictate required collection schedules.

In determining timing of distribution, it is important to know the value timeframe for each performance measure and

Figure 14. Performance Measure Matrix Identifying Specific
                   Relevant Users

Performance Measure	Specific User
BX Line, Activity A, Cycle Time	Bill (front-line supervisor)
BX Line, Activity A, Average Defects Per Unit	Bill (front-line supervisor)
BX Line, Activity B, Cycle Time	Sue (front-line supervisor)
BX Line, Activity B, Average Defects Per Unit	Sue (front-line supervisor)
BX Line, Activity C, Cycle Time	Ted (front-line supervisor)
BX Line, Activity C, Average Defects Per Unit	Ted (front-line supervisor)
BX Line, Total Cycle Time	Mary (line manager)
BX Line, Average Defects Per Unit	Mary (line manager)

A matrix pairing a specific performance measure with a
specific user.

associated user. Performance-related information normally has
value for only a specific amount time. That is why we often
hear someone say, "I could have used that information two
weeks ago. Now it's worthless." As a general rule, the closer
someone is to the action, the more immediate performance-
related information is required.

Normally the more someone is directly
involved in a process or activity,
the more immediate performance-related
information is needed.

In chapter 2, an example was cited from a service company in which front-line supervisors are able to continuously access a computer system to view how customer requests are queuing up. The computer system allows supervisors to instantly determine the amount of elapsed time on any given request. If an unacceptable backlog begins to accumulate, a supervisor can immediately shift work requests to other workers.

How much value would such information be to the front-line supervisors if it was delivered a week later? A day later? Or even an hour later? In this instance, front-line supervisors, who are immediately controlling the action, require performance-related information in basically real time. Their managers, however, probably do not require such immediacy. As such, in determining timeliness of distribution, it is importance to identify who needs what when. In some instances, like the service company supervisors, information may be needed in near real-time. Remember, performance-related information is of little value if it can't be immediately accessed when needed.

Performance-related information is of little
value if delivered too late to the intended user.

As a general rule, when viewing a performance measurement hierarchy, collected measures normally need to be distributed much faster at the base of the hierarchy than at the top of the hierarchy. It is often beneficial to add columns for frequency of collection and timing of distribution to the matrix in Figure 14. This is illustrated in Figure 15.

"How" questions refer to:

- How a specific performance measure is collected.
- How that information is distributed to a specific person.
- How the collected information is displayed (this is discussed in detail in chapter 6).

Answering these questions before developing a matrix similar to that illustrated in Figure 15 is extremely difficult, if not impossible. Therefore, let the developed matrix answering the what, who, and when questions guide your collection and distribution design as well. For example, it is difficult to answer the question, "How do I collect cycle time?" It is much easier to answer the question, "How do I collect work order cycle time for activity B of process X and distribute that information to Mike and Jane on a weekly basis?"

In developing a means for collecting performance measures, always attempt to "piggyback" on an existing system. For example, there may already be a work order log-in system in place for activity B of process X. The existing log-in system already identifies entry and exit times for each work order. The difference (exit time - entry time) represents work order cycle time for activity B. Instead of creating a new cycle time collection system, one simply has to collect the existing work order log-in forms and do some basic subtraction. The next task is to devise the means such that Mike and Jane can receive the information on the needed weekly basis.

When developing a performance measurement collection process, always try to "piggyback" an existing system if possible.

Figure 15. Performance Measure Matrix Including Collection Frequency and Distribution Timing

Performance Measure	Specific User	Collection Frequency	Distribution Timing
BX Line, Activity A, Cycle Time	Bill (front-line supervisor)	Continuous (per unit)	Hourly
BX Line, Activity A, Average Defects Per Unit	Bill (front-line supervisor)	Continuous (per unit)	Hourly
BX Line, Activity B, Cycle Time	Sue (front-line supervisor)	Continuous (per unit)	Hourly
BX Line, Activity B, Average Defects Per Unit	Sue (front-line supervisor)	Continuous (per unit)	Hourly
BX Line, Activity C, Cycle Time	Ted (front-line supervisor)	Continuous (per unit)	Hourly
BX Line, Activity C, Average Defects Per Unit	Ted (front-line supervisor)	Continuous (per unit)	Hourly
BX Line, Total Cycle Time	Mary (line manager)	Continuous (per unit)	Daily
BX Line, Average Defects Per Unit	Mary (line manager)	Continuous (per unit)	Daily

The same matrix as illustrated in Figure 14, but with the addition of "Collection Frequency" and "Distribution Timing" columns.

Also, when developing a collection method, focus on collecting bottom-level performance hierarchy measures first. Frequently, measures higher in a performance hierarchy can simply be summed from lower measures. Remember the cautions associated with such summing, however, as described in chapter 4.

Some companies use a "spoke and hub" system for collecting and distributing performance measures. As illustrated in Figure 16, all collected performance measures are routed to a single hub, representing a single person or department. The information is then distributed to needed users on some predetermined schedule.

Figure 16. A Typical "Spoke and Hub" Performance Measure Collection and Distribution System

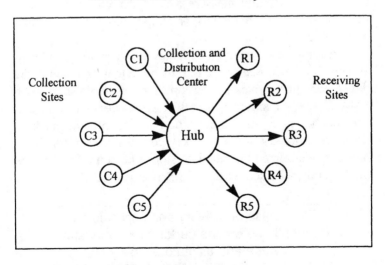

A typical "spoke" and "hub" performance measure collection and distribution system.

_ncreasingly, many companies are using networked, computer-based performance measurement collection and distribution systems. Computer-based systems can collect performance-related information in near-real time and distribute this information electronically to almost everyone simultaneously. Such systems provide process monitoring and enhanced situational awareness capabilities that simply cannot be duplicated or matched with hand-collected or paper distribution systems.

Two final columns may now be added to the matrix started in Figure 14 and expanded in Figure 15. The columns include collection and distribution methods, as illustrated in Figure 17. In most instances, the creation of such a performance measurement matrix is an iterative process. That is, a number of changes and fine-tunings are normal. In some instances, the ability to actually measure a desired performance factor may prove to be impractical or simply too costly or time-consuming.

Creating such a matrix also forces designers to consider all aspects of a performance measurement system. In the end, the developed performance measurement system should be SMART (i.e., specific, measurable, action-oriented, relevant, and timely). In creating a collection and distribution method, timeliness should always be a key consideration. Remember, performance-related information is of little value if it can't be immediately accessed when and where it is needed.

Timeliness of delivery and accessibility frequently determine performance measure value and ultimate usability.

Figure 17. Performance Measure Matrix Including Collection and Distribution Methods

Performance Measure	Specific User	Collection Frequency	Distribution Timing	Collection Method	Distribution Method
BX Line, Activity A, Cycle Time	Bill (front-line supervisor)	Continuous (per unit)	Hourly	Runtime Sensors	Machine Displays
BX Line, Activity A, Average Defects Per Unit	Bill (front-line supervisor)	Continuous (per unit)	Hourly	QA Inspect	QA Reports
BX Line, Activity B, Cycle Time	Sue (front-line supervisor)	Continuous (per unit)	Hourly	Runtime Sensors	Machine Displays
BX Line, Activity B, Average Defects Per Unit	Sue (front-line supervisor)	Continuous (per unit)	Hourly	QA Inspect	QA Reports
BX Line, Activity C, Cycle Time	Ted (front-line supervisor)	Continuous (per unit)	Hourly	Runtime Sensors	Machine Displays
BX Line, Activity C, Average Defects Per Unit	Ted (front-line supervisor)	Continuous (per unit)	Hourly	QA Inspect	QA Reports
BX Line, Total Cycle Time	Mary (line manager)	Continuous (per unit)	Daily	A+B+C Total Time	Printout Analysis
BX Line, Average Defects Per Unit	Mary (line manager)	Continuous (per unit)	Daily	A+B+C Average	QA Reports Analysis

The final completion of the matrix, adding "Collection" and "Distribution" Methods.

SUMMARY

The design and development of any performance measurement collection and distribution system should be guided by first identifying:

- Specific measures to be collected.
- Relevant users.
- Required collection frequencies and timeliness of distribution.

Whenever possible, piggyback on existing information collection and distribution systems to obtain performance-related information. Further, when developing a collection and distribution system, always make sure that *specific* performance-related information is provided to a relevant *user* in a *timely* fashion such that the information actually adds *value* to the operation of a given *process*.

Creating a Performance Measurement System

Step	Description
1	Define needed types of performance-related information that can help achieve desired performance levels.
2	Develop relevant and usable family of measures.
3	Develop specific performance measurement hierarchies.
4	Develop collection and distribution methods that assure timeliness and usability.

CHAPTER 6

Performance Measure Displays

A picture is worth a thousand words.

The final step in creating a performance measurement system is the actual design and development of the performance-related information displays themselves. This is basically the "how should it look" part of the performance measurement process. The goal of any performance measurement display is to provide intended users with relevant and meaningful information that can be quickly assimilated and understood. Performance-related information displays represent the final output of any performance measurement system.

Performance measurement displays should provide relevant and meaningful information that can be quickly and easily assimilated and understood by the intended user.

A dashboard type performance measurement display (illustrated in Figure 18) is often the most valuable. In fact, the cluster

Figure 18. Conceptual Performance Measure Display

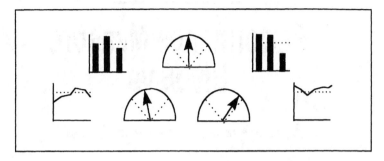

A conceptual performance measure "dashboard."

of displays on your car's dashboard provides some interesting insights and general guidelines for creating performance measurement displays, for example:

- *A quick scan tells all.* The displays on your car's dashboard normally do not require lengthy study to gain needed information. Instead, they are designed in such a way that a quick glance provides most, if not all of the needed information. In creating performance measurement displays, this same principle should be followed. A good display arrangement should quickly provide all critically needed performance-related information. Only if problems are noted, should more in-depth study be required.

- *Information does not have to be further converted.* Think how disconcerting it would be if your speedometer displayed that you were traveling at *17 x 3.53 mph.* You would then have to mentally make one more conversion to learn that you were actually driving about 60 mph. When creating performance measurement displays, make sure that viewers will be able to quickly understand the presented information without having to first convert the data to more meaningful figures.

- *Measurements have associated meanings.* Think for a moment about a temperature gauge on a piece of machinery in a manufacturing factory. You may not know the exact significance of a specific reading. However, the numbers are often associated with something that does have meaning, usually a color-coded system of green (normal), yellow (caution, temperature rising), and red (over heating). As long as the numbers are in the green, even though those numbers may not have specific meaning, you know that everything is fine.

  The same principle applies to performance measurement displays. Always attempt to provide specific meaning to performance metrics by associating them with a desired performance goal (perhaps a simple dashed line) or a color-coded performance range (green for normal, yellow for caution, and red for a problem). The more meaning that can be provided to any performance measurement display, the more beneficial it will be to the intended user.

  When using color-coded schemes, always attempt to use conventional associations. For example, a green-yellow-red combination has meaning to most people. However, a blue-violet-pink combination doesn't. Although creativity and artistic license are encouraged, excesses of creativity may actually detract from the intended message. The goal of any performance measurement system is to provide usable information, and nothing should blur that focus.

- *Fixed positions are provided whenever possible.* What would happen, for example, if every time you glanced at your car's dashboard, the position of a specific display, such as your speedometer, changed? Most of us would agree that such continued repositioning would be quite bothersome. The same concept applies to performance measurement displays. As much as possible, provide some permanency for individual display positions. This allows users to immediately direct their attention to specific information and not waste time searching from chart to chart.

Following the simple principles outlined above will add a great deal of value to any performance measurement displays. An overriding design principle in the creation of performance measurement displays is that they are simple, yet intuitively informative.

> Performance measurement displays
> should be simple yet highly informative
> to the intended user.

GRAPHICAL DISPLAYS

In most instances, a graphical interface composed of various charts and graphs is used in the display of performance measurements. Although specific designs may vary, the following guiding principles should be adhered to:

- Do not make individual charts and graphs too busy. Keep them as simple as possible such that they have immediate meaning to the intended user.

- Use standard types of graphs (e.g., bar charts, pie charts, etc.) that we're all familiar with. In creating various graphs, try to maintain some sort of format consistency.

That is, each graph should not be a unique design in and of itself.

- Use a large enough font and drawing sizes such that graphs and charts can be easily read. Also, make sure that you don't mistakenly fool intended users by adopting various scales. By doing so, a casual glance may indicate that one performance measure is doing much better or worse than another, when in fact, the difference is really due to using different scales.

- As noted earlier, place meaning into graphs and charts by using commonly associated colors (green for normal, yellow for caution, and red for problem) or desired performance goals indicated by a dashed line. When using different colors, make sure that usage is consistent and each color has a specific meaning. That is, don't use red on one graph to indicate a problem and then use it on the next graph to indicate superior performance. Always strive for consistency.

- Check with intended users. Get their feedback and implement their suggestions as much as possible. Remember, the final user is the customer of any performance measurement system.

Consistency, simplicity, understandability, and readability should always guide the creation of any performance measurement display. Excessive creativity may actually distract from the intended user of a performance measure display.

One company for example had a very creative person assigned to developing its performance indicator displays. The individual chose the assignment as an opportunity for artistic expression. Each performance measurement display became an individual piece of art. No two displays ever looked exactly alike. There was no standardization of colors, scale, or format.

Although the end product of such efforts may have been artistically interesting, it had little practical value for harried managers trying to quickly detect any change in performance or identify root causes of a developing problem. Unfortunately, rather than change and standardize the display design process, thereby curbing such artistic license, the company did nothing. As a result, potential users simply ignored the abstract displays, completely bypassing what could have potentially been a very valuable source of performance-related information.

In the next section, a brief look at the organization of performance measurement displays will be offered.

ORGANIZATION

In developing performance measurement displays, always think of who needs what performance-related information when and in what format. One approach is to provide the most critical and/or most frequently used information in the most dominant or proximal position possible. Graphical displays in a notebook format would include this information at the beginning. Conversely, if a "panel" type of display is used, this critical information would most likely appear in the center of the display and be appropriately highlighted. Additional supporting performance-related information would then be linked to this core information. Usually, the supporting information is placed peripherally or around the core information, as shown in Figure 19. This figure illustrates a well developed performance measurement display. Core or critical measures are displayed in the center and encircled by a dashed line. Other measures of less immediate importance are outside the line. A quick glance at the core measures should give a good overall perspective. If problems are indicated, the peripherally displayed performance measures should help identify the problem source.

Figure 19. Core Measures in a Conceptual Performance
          Measure Display

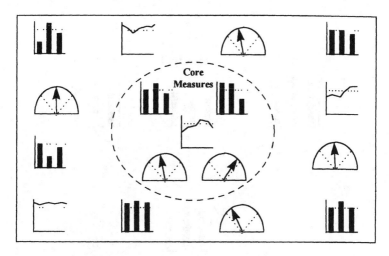

A conceptual performance measure display highlighting
"core" measures in the center.

If supporting performance-related information is used,
always attempt to link it graphically to core information whenever possible. For example, if a critical process cycle time performance measure is based on the combined cycle time
measurements of three included activities, then link this activity-specific information in such a way that the intended user
can quickly access it (see Figure 20). Figure 20 illustrates how
a process-level performance measure (process X), can be
decomposed into three activity-level measures (A, B, and C).
That is, the performance measure of process X is comprised of
the sum of measures from activities A, B, and C.

As noted, computer-based systems are increasingly being
used to capture and display performance-related information. It

Figure 20. Linking Core and Supporting Performance-
Related Information

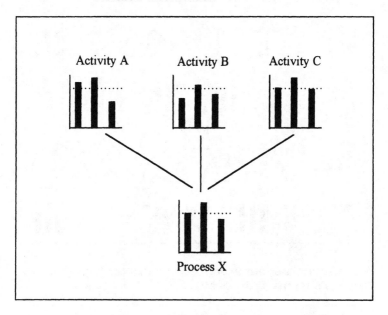

When creating performance measure displays, always try
to link supporting information (such as activity-related
metrics) with more comprehensive measures (such as at
the process level).

is important that designers of such systems avail themselves of
proven techniques specifically related to good graphical user
interface design. A challenge in the design of such computer-
based systems is the organization of the information itself.
Ideally, such performance-related information can be quickly
accessed and linked to other required information. Becoming
"lost" in such computer systems is always a real concern.
Although many of the same principles apply for creating static

displays, additional demands are placed on designers of computer-based systems.

SUMMARY

The final step in the development of a performance measurement system is the actual design of the performance-related information displays. The goal in the development of such displays is to provide specific, relevant, and usable information to the intended user. In addition, this information should be in a format that is easily and rapidly assimilated. Normally graphs and charts are used in displaying performance-related information. In creating such graphics, the challenge is to provide as much meaning as possible, while keeping each individual display as simple as possible. In organizing and displaying performance-related information, a dashboard-type concept is often useful.

Creating a Performance Measurement System

Step	Description
1	Define needed types of performance-related information that can help achieve desired performance levels.
2	Develop relevant and usable family of measures.
3	Develop specific performance measurement hierarchies.
4	Develop collection and distribution methods that assure timeliness and usability.
5	Develop all performance-related information displays.

CHAPTER 7

Putting It All Together

Up-front design equals downstream performance.

A critical enabler in creating and maintaining a high-performance organization is the ability to measure performance. The creation of a performance measurement system is therefore critical to organizational success.

In the previous chapters, the following general steps for creating a performance measurement system were identified:

1. *Define the types of performance-related information needed to help achieve desired performance levels.* Such measures commonly include baseline, trending, control, diagnostic, and planning performance measures. These various measures are not mutually exclusive, and a single performance measure can serve multiple roles. The goal in developing any performance measurement system is to create measures that have real value and meaning.

2. *Develop a relevant and usable family of measures.* Developing a family of measures helps an organization focus on what's really important to its ultimate success. A

family of measures usually represents four to six interrelated but separate key aspects of performance. They normally involve the following types of measures: productivity, quality, timeliness, cycle time, resource utilization, and cost. In many instances, multiple measures of the same family member are collected. For example, a service company may wish to create different types of timeliness measures such as percentage of on-time deliveries and response time of service calls, since timeliness is such an important success factor in satisfying customers.

3. *Develop specific performance measurement hierarchies.* A performance measurement hierarchy consists of different levels of the same performance measure (e.g., cycle times for a specific activity and for the overall process). The creation of a performance measurement hierarchy helps ensure that relevant and meaningful performance-related information is collected and distributed within the right levels of an organization. As noted, providing the right level of information to the right persons at the right time is critical for optimizing overall organizational performance. In creating a performance measurement hierarchy, specific users should always be associated with each measurement level. This practice helps ensure that the right person is receiving the right level of performance-related information.

4. *Develop collection and distribution methods that ensure timeliness and usability.* To achieve relevance, most performance-related information must also have timeliness. Creating collection and distribution methods that provide relevant information to specific users within a required timeframe is critical to the success of any performance measurement system. Increasingly, a usable timeframe

means near real time. Accordingly, computer-based systems have much to offer in the collection and distribution of performance-related measures. When developing collection and distribution strategies, piggyback on existing systems whenever possible.

5. *Develop useful performance-related information displays.* The actual output of any performance measurement system is a graphical display of performance measures. A key success factor in the development of such displays is that they be simple, comprehensible, meaningful, and above all else, usable for the intended users. By incorporating user feedback and needs, better displays can be developed.

By giving careful consideration to the initial design and development of a performance measurement system, more meaningful, usable, and true value-added, performance-related information can be obtained. Always remember the SMART acronym, developing performance measures that are specific, measurable, action-oriented, relevant, and timely.

A review of the following guidelines can help in the design of any performance measurement system.

- *Measurement drives behavior.* This can be either good or bad. Make sure then that you measure the things that will actually help achieve desired performance objectives. Developing bad measures that can be easily manipulated or that lead to unwanted performance outcomes, such as holding team meetings for no real purpose except that the number of team meetings held is being tracked, adds little value to any organization.

- *Measure real work outputs and accomplishments.* Also measure those in-process factors that affect work outputs and accomplishments. Always focus on bottom-line performance, not on unrelated and frequently distracting worker behaviors, such as solemn or complaining employees.

- *Performance measurement systems cost money to develop and maintain.* Focus on capturing these critical few measurements that will actually be used and are important. Create a relevant and organizationally-applicable family of measures and associated performance measurement hierarchies.

- *To ensure usefulness and relevance, tie a specific performance measurement to a specific user by name or position.* An acid test of any performance measurement system should be the ability to identify by name, who uses what information and how it is being used to achieve what supporting organizational goal.

- *Develop measures and associated capture/delivery systems that provide adequate warnings of negative changes.* To have relevance, such information must also have timeliness. That is, it can't be delivered or gathered "after the fact." Remember, a good performance measurement system provides the right kind of information to the right person at the right time and in the right format.

- *Performance measurement displays should be easily and quickly understandable.* Keep displays simple, specific, and relevant. Graphical formats are best.

Finally, here are the keys to creating an effective performance measure:

- The measure has specific use to a real individual or group of individuals. An effective performance measure will always help people monitor, control, manage, track, diagnose, improve, or plan some aspect of their work better. If this first usability attribute is not met, a performance measure by definition cannot be considered to have real value. In creating any performance measure, it is imperative to specifically identify the intended users and how the performance measure will be specifically used. Keep it simple. If you can't identify a specific user and use, you won't have a good performance measure.

- The performance measure is captured and delivered to the intended user within a predetermined period. Because timeliness is an important attribute of usability, a good performance measure must be delivered at the right time such that it can actually be used. A bad performance measure arrives late or after the fact. As such, it has little value or applicability. For example, a project may be on an extremely tight budget, requiring constant monitoring of spent funds. If the project manager cannot access current spending levels, he cannot properly manage the project, assuring that it will be completed within the allotted budget.

- The performance measure is distributed to the right person at the right time, or can be easily accessed by the right person. Just as performance-related information must have timeliness, it must also have a specific identified user who needs the information. Getting performance-related information to the wrong person is unacceptable.

- A performance measure's meaning can be quickly and easily grasped and understood. For example, subtle changes in performance levels or developing problems associated with a specific process or operation can be easily and quickly spotted. A good performance measure, therefore, should not require extensive study to grasp its significance. A performance measure also contains some type of comparative basis that quickly allows the intended user to compare and contrast acceptable or desired performance levels with current performance levels.

- The display of performance measures should conform to standardized guidelines. For example, the use of the color red should have the same meaning in the display of all performance measures. It should not indicate bad on one display and good on another. A good performance measure display will conform to some set of predetermined guidelines, thereby enhancing understandability and usability.

Further Reading

Cycle Time Reduction, Jerry L. Harbour, Ph.D., Quality Resources, 1996.

Everyone's Problem Solving Handbook, Michael R. Kelly, Quality Resources, 1992.

Handbook for Productivity Measurement and Improvement, William Christopher and Carl Thor, eds., Productivity Press, 1993 (includes several articles by Carl Thor).

Keeping Score, Mark Graham Brown, Quality Resources, 1996.

Measuring, Managing, and Maximizing Performance, Will Kaydos, Productivity Press, 1991.

Process Reengineering Handbook, Jerry L. Harbour, Ph.D., Quality Resources, 1994.